GREENHOUSE GARDENING

The Easy & Complete Beginner's Guide to Discover How to Easily Build A Perfect and Inexpensive Own Greenhouse to Growing Healthy Plants, Fruits, And Vegetables All-Year-Round

BOB MAYERS

TABLE OF CONTENTS

Chapter 5

Setting the Environment

Chapter 6

Equipment and Tools

Chapter 7

Growing in the Greenhouse

Chapter 8

How to Grow Plants and Flowers

INTRODUCTION

A greenhouse is a great way to grow plants all year round, and with the right technique, preparation and knowledge you can grow some amazing plants. It's a much-needed respite from Canadians who are blessed with four seasons, but not always with favorable weather. Greenhouses are an excellent way to enjoy garden-fresh produce that tastes better than what you get at most grocery stores. Here's how to get started in the wonderful world of greenhouse gardening:

1. Pick your spot for your new greenhouse. The best place for a greenhouse is in a sunny spot that does not get hit by the chilly winds. A greenhouse can be built almost anywhere, but it needs a bit of flat ground and enough space. Remember that the bigger the greenhouse, the bigger the plants you can grow in it.

2. You will need to dig down several feet to make room for supporting posts. If you are building your first greenhouse, this is where most people make mistakes. It is much easier to build on an existing floor rather than trying to dig down several feet. Unless you already have dug out the land, looking into laying bricks or concrete slabs is a good idea if you'd like your own greenhouse floor.

3. You will need to decide on the size of your greenhouse. Greenhouse kits are widely available at most home improvement stores, but you can also get one-of-a-kind greenhouses by incorporating windows and an insulated roof into a structure built on your property.

4. Greenhouse kits vary in size and price, but materials required for construction are consistent between all kits. Materials necessary for construction include 2x4's to build the walls, wood

or metal framing materials for the frame of your choice, screws or nails to secure the framing

materials to the walls, and 4x8 sheets of plastic that will become the roof and walls.

5. The next step in greenhouse construction is erecting the framework. Depending on your budget, you can secure 2x4's to plywood sheets and then use the resulting panel as a frame, or you can also have professionals construct your frame for you. If you choose to build only one wall, it is important to erect it while it is still warm out so that it will adjust itself after cooling down. If your greenhouse will not have an attached floor, make sure you allow an additional foot of height for snow accumulation.

6. You will need to decide how much light will be allowed through your greenhouse. Greenhouse panels are available at most home improvement stores in various sizes and strengths (in case of strong winds). Panels are made of different materials as well and each one has a specific function. One common material used in greenhouse panels is Polycarbonate, which transmits light and keeps out the heat. It is resistant to snow, hail, and bad weather, but be aware that it easily scratches so you will need to handle it with care. Greenhouse panels can also be made

of glass or acrylic, which is a much more expensive option but gives you the clearest view of plants.

7. You will also need to decide what kind of door or doorway you would like to have. There are several options available such as sliding doors that allow for easy access, double swing doors that open outward or inward, and even doors with windows.

There are many more to learn and this book will help you learn how to start with your first garden.

Chapter 1

WHY BUILDING A GREENHOUSE?

Plants can be majorly cultivated using 3 different systems of cultivation; these are the in-ground system, greenhouse system, or hydroponic system of cultivation. While there is no technicality involved in the in-ground system, the greenhouse and hydroponic systems both have certain advantages over the in-ground system. Virtually any kind of plant can be cultivated in a greenhouse, but with careful selection of the plants to be grown, profit can be maximized. There are times it becomes too windy, too dark, too cold, too hot, or too rainy and it takes a miracle for plants, especially vegetables, to survive such climatic conditions. Greenhouse growers have no headache whenever the climatic condition becomes adverse because it has always been their responsibility to control the environmental condition in their greenhouse garden. The benefits are as follows:

OUT OF SEASON PRODUCTION

This is perhaps the major reason many growers dabble into this system of gardening. Greenhouse gardening offers you the benefit of a longer growing season, that is, plants can be grown all year-round in a greenhouse. When "out of season" crops are made available, there is usually a huge rise in their selling prices when there is high market demand, and it consequently yields a high-profit return on the investment made. Therefore, you must carry out adequate research about the plant to be cultivated before investing in its "out of season" production. Some growers call this stage the preliminary research stage, it is to ensure that the investment you are about to make will be profitable at the end of the day. In greenhouse gardening, the plants grow faster and healthier, and therefore, can be made available early before their season, during their season, and also when they are out of season. The extended growing season is one of the major benefits derived from greenhouse gardening.

HIGHER YIELD

When the greenhouse system of gardening is compared to the traditional open-field cultivation, the yield from a greenhouse is usually 10 times higher in quantity and quality. Although this depends on the size of a greenhouse used, also the type of plant being cultivated, and the environmental condition provided in the greenhouse if optimum. The plants in a greenhouse usually have little or no enemy such as plant diseases to fight against and so it is easy for them to grow healthily and germinate quickly. The favorable environmental condition that plants enjoy in the greenhouse is a stimulant for healthy growth and higher yield. This particular benefit from using a greenhouse is being utilized in many countries of the world where the population is constantly on the increase to ensure that there is enough food in circulation that will meet the needs of the teeming population.

HIGHER QUALITY

Another benefit that is derived from using a greenhouse system is that it gives quality yield at the end of each growing season. As stated earlier that the yield from a greenhouse is usually 10 times higher than open field cultivation in quantity and also in quality. Using a greenhouse for your plant cultivation will not only offer you the benefit of producing more yield from your cultivation but you can also be assured that the product you will obtain will be of great quality. Higher yield and higher quality are benefits enjoyed by practicing greenhouse gardening.

PLANT/CROP RELIABILITY

Due to the absence of pests, diseases, and other plant infections in a greenhouse, the plants cultivated in the greenhouse have increased reliability. That is, there is a reduced risk of infection and the yield from the greenhouse cultivation can be trusted as clean and healthy. Also, unlike conventional gardening, the grower remains unbothered during adverse climatic conditions because the plants in the greenhouse are totally not affected by the external bad weather. The reliability of plant healthy growth is high in a greenhouse system.

PEST AND DISEASE-FREE PRODUCTION

A greenhouse makes it easy to protect the plants being cultivated from pest attacks and keep them free from diseases. A good and strong greenhouse should, however, be purchased to easily achieve this and keep pests away from the plants. The protection provided by the greenhouse is another great benefit that gives the plants cultivated through this method an edge over the plants cultivated using the conventional open field.

PROVIDES THE PLANTS WITH OPTIMUM GROWING CONDITION

This is another benefit that plants in a greenhouse enjoy as they are provided with the optimum growing condition, and therefore, they grow faster, better, and healthier. Providing the best growing environment for your plants is a jackpot that harnesses the highest possible growth rate of the plants. Regardless of the plants being cultivated, the greenhouse provides the grower with the opportunity to supply the plants with a favorable and optimum growing environment. This growing environment can sometimes mean trapping beneficial insects inside the greenhouse because not all insects are harmful to the plants. Some are very beneficial and while these beneficial insects can come and go as they like in an open field system, an advantage of using a greenhouse is that they can be trapped inside, and therefore, continuously enhance the growth of the plants in the greenhouse.

ABSENCE OF TOXIC PESTICIDES

In the traditional system of gardening, there is sometimes the need for the strong application of toxic pesticides to fight against certain pest attacks. These toxic pesticides, no matter how little, usually reflect on the yield at the end of the day but the good news is that there is usually no need for such application of pesticides in a greenhouse. This keeps the plants in the greenhouse fresh and also ensures a clean yield at the end of the growing season. This benefit also makes it possible to produce genetically superior transplants.

ENERGY-SAVING AND LESS LABOR-INTENSIVE

In a greenhouse, the application of water, light, nutrient, etc. is totally controlled by the grower. This makes it easy to control how they are supplied, unlike in conventional gardening where it is more difficult to conserve energy. The ability to conserve energy in a greenhouse helps to improve the environment at large. Greenhouse gardening also makes gardening an interesting thing to do. It makes gardening less labor-intensive and almost completely stress-free. This realization is perhaps the reason we have more home growers lately as many growers practice greenhouse gardening just for the fun of it, or better still, as a hobby.

Other benefits of using a greenhouse include the efficient utilization of nutrients, water, pesticide (if any), and also the bridging of gap in plant cultivation that exist as a result of bad climatic conditions and the presence of non-arable lands in most areas.

Chapter 2

TYPES OF GREENHOUSES

I t is very important that you choose and build a greenhouse that is right for your property so that it can take advantage of the maximum amount of available sunlight. This all depends on selecting the proper greenhouse structure. I will be giving you a detailed description of all the greenhouse types out there and their disadvantages and advantages.

ATTACHED

Before you choose a shape, you need to think about whether you want to build a freestanding or attached greenhouse. What are these, and how are they different?

Just like the name says, this kind of greenhouse will be attached to your house. One of the pros of having this type of greenhouse is you won't be using as many building materials as you would for a freestanding one.

The ventilation and heating tools could be used for your house, too. It does come with some drawbacks in terms of trying to control the temperature inside the greenhouse. The building that the greenhouse is attached to could shade the greenhouse and limit the amount of light that the plants need.

The attached greenhouses could be in two different shapes: even-span and lean-to.

A lean-to greenhouse is normally set up so that it is on the south-facing side of your house. The ridge of its roof will connect to the house. This kind of greenhouse is cheap and easy to heat, especially if you are in colder climates.

Even-span greenhouses will give you more space for more plants. How? The end wall will be attached to a house, and its rafters will be the same length. One con of this kind of greenhouse is the cost of the building and heating the inside as compared to the lean-to.

Because of this, you could just put the money into a freestanding greenhouse but don't forget that electricity and water can be reached easily when a greenhouse is attached to another building.

Basically, both even-span and lean-to greenhouses can have the same problems, and that is shadowing. The shadow of the building that the greenhouse is attached to will always cause a reduction in the amount of sunlight.

WINDOW-FARM

This is an indoor, vertical garden that lets you grow plants in just about any window. It allows the plants to used natural sunlight. You will be using the same heating and cooling system as you do for your living space; all you need to do is add some organic liquid soil. This is a type of hydroponic farming.

This type of system is completely DIY. It is the best way for people to grow fresh produce, no matter where they live. You don't need a yard. The cheapest option is a starter kit that can be found online for under $200.

Since it is a hydroponic system, it will require more components like nutrients, tubes, and pumps and more maintenance than a normal soil-based greenhouse.

FREESTANDING GREENHOUSES

These are similar to the attached ones, and they can also be lean-to or even-span-shaped. Let's compare these two and move on to describe other types of freestanding ones.

Even-Span

This type of greenhouse can be characterized by the rafters that are equally spaced, the roof trusses, and the building will support itself. There are many kinds available at most home improvement warehouses, or you can find them online. Most of these will allow you to choose between two types of coverings: 10 mm. polycarbonate or 3 mm. tempered glass.

This kind of structure can be easily recognized by the gable, which is a triangle between the sloped roof sides. This is the most common kind of greenhouse since it uses the most amount of sun.

It also has a lot of space inside that lets you grow various plants while keeping the optimal conditions. Even-span kinds usually require glass panels that run from the ground to the top and an aluminum frame for more support.

Uneven-Span

This is the total opposite of the one above since the rafters will always be unequal, and it doesn't support itself. This is the best choice if you have a hill that you would like to use for something.

The best advantage of this kind of greenhouse is all the sunlight that it utilizes. The biggest disadvantage is the problems working inside because of the limited space and how it is configured.

Hoop House

This can be easily identified by its curved roof or military-style hut design. These hoops are normally made from PVC or aluminum pipes and then covered with polyethylene panels or film to give them some insulation. Basically, this means that you will stretch a piece of plastic over a series of hoops. It could also be made using straight lines by using elbows for the PVC pipes to get the shape you want. This is the least expensive design of all the greenhouses. The construction would cost about one dollar per square foot.

The sidewalls will be very low, and this limits your headroom and storage space. This is the easiest and cheapest kind to build, and that is why most people like it. You can get it on most online shops for about $200 or even build one yourself.

A hoop house is useful because any type of precipitation will just roll off the roof easily. It is best for crops that grow low to the ground like strawberries or lettuce. You could use it to grow cucumbers and tomatoes.

Hoop houses aren't always cheap. If you love this shape and want to use the best type of materials, you can find them online. For a bit more money, you can get double-walled paneling that will last for ten years.

These are relatively easy to construct and can be adapted to small amounts of land. This shape is not as sturdy as an A-frame or the post and rafter.

Gothic Arch

This kind of greenhouse is very aesthetically pleasing. This design can be easily identified by its walls being bent over to make a pointed roof that was inspired by the windows in Gothic cathedrals found around the world. It has a semicircular frame that is normally made from conduit or galvanized pipe. It is usually covered with plastic sheeting.

This kind of greenhouse is very wide and would be great for anybody who would like to grow their plants in rows. You can put plants on the shelves plus hang some pots inside as well. It is similar to the hoop house above and has the same functionally.

It conserves heat well. Its shape makes sure that snow will just slide off without accumulating on top. There are several different models to choose from, and make sure you research to find the one best for your climate.

The pros of this greenhouse are its efficient and simple design. Using plastic sheeting lowers the overall cost a lot. The design shape lets snow and water runoff easily.

It has some cons as the sidewalls' height is very low, which restricts the headroom and storage space.

A-Frame

For me, this is the easiest and simplest greenhouse to set up, and it is charming. Its design allows you to save money on construction materials and is perfect for a tiny backyard.

All you have to do is to put short sidewalls and the roof together to form a triangular shape. The biggest problem that you might run into is the poor air circulation in its corners.

It is one of the more popular designs. The most significant advantage is its simple design and the fact that it doesn't use many materials. The typical coverings would be glass, but translucent, rigid polycarbonate panels can be used, and some kits come with this type of covering.

The pros of this kind of greenhouse are its simple design and the use of fewer materials. Some cons are its narrow sidewall that limits the functionality of using the whole greenhouse. Air circulation could be a problem in the corners.

Post and Rafter

These are probably the most popular since most gardeners go for this kind. The construction is very simple and is the strongest out there. The structure is very practical, too. Because this design is a bit top-heavy, the frame needs to be footed. This will increase the cost as compared to the other designs.

This greenhouse uses heat and space very efficiently. With this greenhouse, you can cut down significantly on heat loss during the winter months. Again, do some research online, and you might find one that you just have to have. Some designs even have a built-in gutter system so you can collect rainwater runoff if it is allowed in your area.

Its rafters give the roof more support during the winter months, but it might make the entire construction heavier, and this will require a stronger frame that might cost more. If you do decide on this type of greenhouse, make sure you create a foundation for it.

The most common coverage options are normally glass, but rigid translucent polycarbonate panels can make the cost a lot lower. Its pros are its simple design, maximum space usage along the walls. It has better air circulation, especially along the walls. It does require more materials like metal and wood than other designs.

Mini Portable

These are just like their name says: they are portable and small. They aren't large enough for you to get inside and are covered simply. They usually have some shelves to optimize the light and heat inside an enclosed outdoor area or your house.

Most of these are covered with plastic sheeting since they are portable and don't need to be excessively heavy. This keeps them lightweight and easily moveable if you need to.

Their small size makes them a good option for people who don't have a lot of floor space but want to have a greenhouse. They are easy to build and very affordable.

These greenhouses are not very sturdy and are too small for anyone who wants to be serious gardeners. You won't be able to grow too many plants in one of these small greenhouses.

Tabletop Greenhouse

These are a simple DIY kind of greenhouse if you are very creative, and you don't have a lot of space in your home, but you want a safe place to keep and grow plants. They are very unique and pretty since you can make them from various materials and don't have one design. These can be made from old shadow boxes, picture frames, fish bowls, and a lot more. You could purchase some that have already been made.

These are normally made from panels of plastic, acrylic, or glass. The frames could be made from various materials depending on the look you want. They normally don't need covers other than what was mentioned bit if you put them in a cold space, you could use some plastic sheeting.

These treasures are affordable, compact, and used for decorative purposes, but they can absolutely keep a plant alive. With various DIY designs out there, you can have as many of these tiny treasures as you want.

Chapter 3

PLANNING YOUR PROJECT

There are a lot of considerations to be made before you buy a greenhouse. Obviously, there is a budget, but other factors may well influence your budget. If you live in a particularly cold area, then double glazing and heating are important, but in a hotter area, the primary considerations would be airflow and ventilation.

WHAT SIZE TO BUY

Bigger is not always best, but many people aspire to a large greenhouse. What size to buy will depend on the space you have available plus what you are planning to grow. Of course, no matter what size you buy when you start to use it you will run out of space and wish you'd bought a bigger one!

If you are buying a second-hand greenhouse or picking one up for free, then you have less choice in size and will usually make do with whatever comes up.

The most common size is 8x6" though you can get slightly smaller ones and very much larger ones. This is a good starter size, but you need to be aware that your space is limited and you will struggle to fit a lot in. However, it is a great size for starting off seeds and growing a few tomatoes or chili plants.

Check any local planning or zoning regulations before you buy a greenhouse. If you are on an allotment, then check their rules too. The last thing you want is to put up your new greenhouse only to find you have breached a rule and then have to take it down. On allotments, you often need written permission for a greenhouse and to position it in a certain way. As to HOA's, their rules are anyone's guess so check and be certain.

I would recommend visiting a shop that sells greenhouses and walking into a few different sizes. This will help you to visualize the space better and work out which one is best for you. Just remember to avoid the salesperson's charm, or you may end up with a very expensive greenhouse!

When looking for a greenhouse, you need to consider how easy it is for you to maintain and use the greenhouse. If your greenhouse takes a lot of time to maintain each year, then it means less time doing other jobs.

That's the greenhouse I inherited which, as you can see, is a marvel of British engineering. Quite how it is still standing is beyond me as I understand it is well over 20 years old, but it shows what can be made with a bit of creativity!

POSITIONING YOUR GREENHOUSE

Where you will put your greenhouse can influence the size, as well as other factors. Obviously, you need to position it, so it gets good sun throughout the day.

Avoid the north-facing slopes as the amount of light will not be sufficient. Do not build your greenhouse at the bottom of a slope as it is likely to be the location of a frost pocket, meaning cold air will gather around your greenhouse. This makes your greenhouse colder, requiring more heating and reducing the benefits you get from your greenhouse.

Though if you have no choice but to site your greenhouse facing north that is still better than not having a greenhouse at all!

Depending on your preference you may choose to align your greenhouse in one of two ways.

Firstly, you can align it so the sun tracks down one side of the greenhouse. The advantage of this is that one side gets lots of sunlight and the other gets less, allowing you to grow plants that require less sun or need a bit of shade on the side of the greenhouse furthest from the sun.

Alternatively, you can align your greenhouse, so the sun shines on one of the small ends so the whole greenhouse gets sun throughout the day.

Which you choose is up to you, and it may be that the locations available to you in your vegetable plot influence the alignment.

As an 8x6" greenhouse is virtually square, the alignment to the sun is not so important. For larger greenhouses, it does become more important to ensure you maximize the sun for your plants.

Something else to consider is the direction of the prevailing wind in your area. Typically, you will position the door away from the wind. This helps secure your greenhouse and makes it a little less susceptible to wind damage. We will talk more about protecting your greenhouse from wind damage later in this book.

You want to position your greenhouse where it is not under trees. Should the trees lose branches, then it will damage or even destroy your greenhouse.

Ideally, you want your greenhouse located in a sheltered spot where it is not going to be subjected to high winds. This may not always be possible, but if you can do this, then it will help prevent damage in the future.

If you are planning on using an irrigation system or installing electricity, then your choice of the site needs to take this into consideration. It needs to be somewhere that you can supply these services to without too much work or expense. If not, then you are stuck watering by hand and using paraffin or solar heaters like most gardeners!

CHOOSING THE BEST FLOOR

All of these decisions need making before you buy your greenhouse and this is probably one of the most controversial!

Which floor you choose will depend a lot on what you are planning on growing in your greenhouse and your environment.

Your choices are:

- No floor, just use the soil

- The concrete path down the middle, soil to either side

- The concrete path down the middle, weed membrane on either side

- Complete concrete floor

They all have their pros and cons, but it is a personal decision based on your site, budget, and available resources.

The picture is the inside of my inherited greenhouse. It contains a central paved path with a weed membrane on either side on it laid on the soil.

The problem with this is that the weed membrane does not extend outside of the greenhouse, meaning the hard-to-reach edges become infested with weeds. This is okay on the left-hand side but the right-hand side has staged in place so is extremely hard to weed.

The lesson has been learned, and on my next greenhouse, the inside will be much more weed-proof! But back to choosing the best floor for your greenhouse.

The first option is by far the easiest because you don't need to do anything. The downside of this is the weeds will love the heat in the greenhouse and will thrive. You will have a lot of weeding to do, and this can be very awkward to do when the plants are fully grown.

Some people do grow directly into the soil using bottomless pots. Just be aware that although this option is cheap, you will be battling weeds inside your greenhouse as well as outside. You also run the risk of introducing soil-borne pests and diseases if you do not change the topsoil in your greenhouse every year or two.

Having a paved path down the middle of your greenhouse is great as it helps with access and isn't too expensive. You can leave the soil bare on either side or cover it with a weed membrane.

This method works well, as when you put staging in your greenhouse, it becomes very hard to weed underneath it.

Putting weed membrane down will be effective in keeping the weeds away providing you use a decent quality membrane. Expect to replace it every 2 to 5 years, depending on what you use as it will perish and eventually allow weeds through.

The final option is by far the best but is also the most expensive as you have to buy paving slabs for the whole greenhouse or poured concrete. With a larger greenhouse this can soon become expensive. It is also more work as you have to lay sand and hardcore as well as level the paving.

The advantage of this method is that it is a low-maintenance solution. When done properly with a weed membrane under the sand, you should get years of a weed-free greenhouse.

As everything will be in pots, you can also move your plants around so you can reposition them as necessary to get them more or less sun as required.

GLASS VS. POLYCARBONATE PANES

Again, this is a personal preference, and both types of panels have their good and bad points.

Glass is the more expensive solution, and the most fragile, panels can get broken by accident or vandals and need replacing.

However, glass technology is quite advanced, and you can get some great thermally insulated glass which is ideal for colder areas or heated greenhouses.

Most greenhouses use horticultural glass which typically comes in 2' square panels so you can end up with overlapping panels. The disadvantage of this type of glass is that it breaks easily into very jagged and sharp pieces. Because of the size, the panels come in you overlap them, and over time this can become dirty and grow algae, which looks unsightly.

You can buy specially toughened glass for your greenhouse, meaning it isn't going to shatter from a simple touch. It is still breakable, but it will survive an impact from a football though a more solid ball will break it. Just be careful of the edges of toughened glass as that is its weak point. When handling this make sure you never let the edges touch a rough surface.

Plastic or polycarbonate panels are much cheaper to buy and for most applications just as good as glass. The big advantage is that they are a lot harder break which is important if you have kids as accidents do happen.

Because the polycarbonate panels are much lighter than glass, they are also more susceptible to wind damage. In high winds, they can flex and pop out of the frame!

Glass is much heavier and gives your greenhouse a more rigid structure, something that is lacking with polycarbonate panels.

Many polycarbonate panels are slightly opaque, meaning you cannot see in or out clearly. This may not bother you, but some people don't like it, and it can reduce the amount of sunlight your plants get.

You should also be aware that most polycarbonate panels are twin-walled, meaning there are two sheets of plastic with an air gap in the middle. Over time water seeps into this gap and algae forms, which you cannot remove. This has an impact on how much light gets into your greenhouse and also looks untidy. Surprisingly, polycarbonate can cost even more than toughened glass!

Both are easy to get your hands on, being available in many glaziers. My personal preference is the plastic panels purely from the point of view that they are harder to break and less likely to smash if people throw stones at them. However, if I were to heat my greenhouse, then I would look at glass panels for better insulation and heat retention.

Chapter 4

BUILDING YOUR GREENHOUSE

If you're planning to grow food in your backyard or in a small space, building your own greenhouse is the perfect solution. This book will walk you through the process of how to build a greenhouse from scratch, with step-by-step instructions as follows:

STEP 1: UNDERSTANDING GREENHOUSE PRINCIPLES BEFORE BUILDING

One must begin by understanding greenhouse principles before building. This may sound difficult, but it is a valuable step. A greenhouse can be built in countless ways, and different designs may work best for your backyard or even a newly purchased urban lot. However, it is important to consider the following before you begin:

Solar Orientation: A greenhouse that is oriented towards the sun gives off most heat during the day, while one that is oriented away from the sun receives most of its heat at night. This allows for a more comfortable growing environment during warmer months, as well as an ideal climate for winter plantings.

Protecting Plants from UV Rays: Plants can handle temperatures ranging from 60 to 77°F (15 to 25°C) but not beyond that range. UV rays start to affect plants at about 100°F (38°C). Optimum temperatures for a greenhouse are 70°F (21°C) during the day and 35°F (2.5°C) at night.

Insulation: Insulation is needed to keep heating costs lower for your greenhouses. Insulating the ceiling will also allow you to fit more solar panels on the roof without having to close in the space between them. The insulation material should be sprayed around the outside of all walls and the plant leaves in the summer months, as these areas are warmer than other parts of the greenhouse, which is why they lose heat faster.

STEP 2: SELECTING THE RIGHT BUILDING MATERIAL

You should be able to choose the right building material based on the greenhouse's size, the amount of space you have available, and how much money you want to spend. Some good options for your greenhouse include:

Papercrete, a lightweight building material made of cornstarch and water. This is a good choice if your home is close to an urban area with plenty of land at very little cost.

Wood: If you have wood for your greenhouse, then you can build it out of anything from pressure-treated lumber to cedar (although it will likely require staining). Building with wood will be relatively inexpensive and provide a sturdy structure that should last many years.

Polycarbonate: Polycarbonate will prevent insect damage, which is common in some areas, and may be a good choice if weight is an issue. This resin can be formed into rolls and then attached to a frame.

Exterior grade plywood: Plywood is stiffer than other board products but will still work well for a greenhouse as long as it's made of exterior grade plywood. It may not hold up as well in extreme weather conditions but will still work if you design it properly. If you choose to go with a glass greenhouse, then you must decide whether you want single or double pane windows. For greenhouses that are less than 600 square feet (56 square meters) in size, single-pane windows are sufficient.

STEP 3: PLANNING YOUR GREENHOUSE AND PREPARING FOR CONSTRUCTION

After you have determined how you want to build your greenhouse, it's time to plan your greenhouse and prepare for construction. If you're building from the ground up, then planning is simple. However, if you are converting a shed or other structure into a greenhouse, then it will be more difficult because there may be less room to maneuver than if you were building from scratch. The most important thing when converting a structure is that the roofing materials are waterproof and supported with proper drainage below the decking materials.

Designing an efficient layout will improve your greenhouse's performance by 100%. Measurements should be exact so that walls fit together tightly with no gaps in between them. To ensure that a greenhouse is structurally sound, use a combination of framing materials. You should also consider the design of your home's existing foundation before building the greenhouse.

Placing a greenhouse on a basement level is an excellent way to avoid spiders, ants, and other insects that are attracted to heat. However, you will need to make sure that the greenhouse is above ground level so that it does not flood during periods of heavy rain or melting snow.

Adding an extra attic space or floor area to your home can greatly increase the area available for greenhouses and other outdoor facilities such as livestock pens and composting areas. It may also save you money because modifications can be made to the existing foundation instead of adding new ones.

STEP 4: PREPARING YOUR FOUNDATION

Once you have planned your greenhouse and found the right location for it, it's time to prepare your foundation. The most important thing to remember is that the foundation, floor, decking, and roof should all be waterproof. If they are not properly waterproofed, then heat will escape through them and the greenhouse will cost too much to keep warm.

STEP 5: BUILDING YOUR FRAME

The frame must be strong enough to support the weight of snow that may accumulate on the roof in winter. Building this structure can be a bit tricky but there are many online tutorials such as this one from Agriculture Canada to help guide you through the process. To ensure that the frame is strong enough, use a combination of materials such as pressure-treated plywood, 2x6s, and 2x4s.

STEP 6: INSULATION

The walls of a glass greenhouse can deteriorate after a few years because the weather affects them so much. To avoid this, you should insulate the walls with foam board insulation that has been covered with stucco or cement plaster and sealed to keep moisture from seeping in.

STEP 7: BUILDING YOUR ROOF

The roof is one of the most important parts of your greenhouse--not only does it protect crops from harsh weather but it also helps maintain their temperature during the day in summer. To make sure that it is well insulated and waterproof, use 2x6s and 2x4s as your roofing materials.

STEP 8: PLACING THE ROOF ON THE FRAME

The roof will protect crops from rain, snow, sun, and pests. Most greenhouses have clapboard or plywood roofs that can easily be replaced if they become worn out. Before you place a roof on your greenhouse, make sure you measure it precisely using a level to prevent any gaps between the walls and subsequently leaks.

STEP 9: INSTALLING WINDOWS AND VENTILATING DOORS

Windows or doors should be installed at intervals around the exterior of your greenhouse to provide sunlight, airflow, ventilation, light and reduce heat loss.

STEP 10: ADDING FLOORS AND FINISHING TOUCHES

The floors of your greenhouse should be waterproof and made from materials such as pressure-treated plywood, hardwood, or concrete. It is also important to remember that the floor should slope towards a drainage system so that excess water can be redirected away from the greenhouse. When you are building windows, ensure that you leave a gap between the frame and windowpane to prevent moisture from seeping in.

Chapter 5
SETTING THE ENVIRONMENT

Once you've set up your greenhouse, it's time to do what it was supposed to do-foster quick and safe plant growth within it. A greenhouse's strength lies in the ability to control indoor climate conditions.

Temperature is one of those essential climatic conditions. If you want to achieve optimum plant growth, you need to have the right temperature. Light is another significant factor. Remember that one climate factor can influence another. For example, too much sunlight can increase the indoor temperature beyond the appropriate levels inside the greenhouse.

HEAT

If the winters in your area are on the harsh side, or if you want to get a head start on seed germination before spring, you will need to consider adding in heating for your greenhouse.

Electrical heaters today are a lot more energy efficient than they used to be. The most important thing when it comes to choosing your heater is that it should have a thermostat—this helps to keep the temperature constant and makes the whole system more energy-efficient as the heater is turned off when the desired temperature has been reached.

VENTILATION

With two forms of ventilation in mind, each greenhouse should be built-natural and artificial ventilation. For natural ventilation, only a number of outlets and inlets need to be properly positioned to allow natural airflow into and out of the greenhouse. Electricity may or may not be used, but it would only be used to control inlets or outlets opening and closing. Although natural ventilation is a great cost saver, in areas with high outdoor temperatures, it is inefficient.

And that's where there's automatic ventilation. Auto ventilation controls indoor temperatures with louvers and exhaust fans powered by electricity. The distinction between automatic ventilation and natural ventilation powered by electricity is that the former is typically part of a larger air conditioning system that senses temperature and allows the louvers and fans to do so.

COOLING

A different approach is required when ventilation alone is inadequate to manage the temperature within the greenhouse. Two common thermal control strategies that can increase ventilation are fog systems and pad-and-fan systems.

To spread a cooling fog uniformly, fog systems use nozzles mounted every 50 to 100 feet in the greenhouse. It is expensive because it is necessary to use clean water to prevent blocking the tiny mouth of each nozzle.

For automatic ventilation, pad-and-fan technology goes hand in hand. For air inlets, evaporative pads are installed, and the air entering the greenhouse is cooled. In the end, the cool air circulates within the greenhouse, collecting heat before the exhaust fans take it out.

Without proper ventilation and air circulation, your plants are more vulnerable to attack by fungus and mold. You should only cut off the air supply in the very coldest weather.

Air circulation helps to keep the temperature in the room constant in summer and prevents your plants from being stifled.

The general rule is that you need at least two ventilators for every 6 feet in length.

GREENHOUSE VENTILATION—WHY IS IT IMPORTANT?

In order to create an optimal atmosphere, a number of factors must be addressed in your greenhouse. One of the most important climatic variables is air quality. But you might wonder, "Why is my greenhouse ventilation so important?" There are a number of reasons for this. The plants will not grow as fast without proper ventilation, and what they produce will be inferior. Proper ventilation can help to keep your greenhouse climate to a degree that is best suited to the plants you cultivate.

Ventilation greatly affects environmental conditions in your greenhouse. Such factors affect the ability of the plant to perform photosynthesis. This process involves the ability of the plant to transform sunlight into chemical energy. The plant uses this energy to provide it with fuel to grow. This includes the ability of the plant to take important elements from the soil and complete the cycle of reproduction.

Proper greenhouse ventilation will help control the circulation of air, temperature, and humidity.

These factors significantly affect the ability of plants to grow productively. This will help to provide the required amount of carbon dioxide for your plants to grow.

In order to produce photosynthesis, plants need carbon dioxide to perform proper chemical reactions. As carbon dioxide levels begin to decrease the plant's ability to grow, they decrease. Proper ventilation in your greenhouse can help to keep carbon dioxide levels at the amount needed to grow healthily.

We absorb carbon dioxide as the plants grow and produce oxygen. But many people do not know that oxygen is required for plants to grow. Their roots require oxygen from the fresh air. The roots need oxygen to expand, and this is directly related to the ability of the plant to take nutrients from the soil.

HUMIDITY

The humidity here refers to the amount of moisture in the greenhouse-growing environment. It is no news that keeping the wrong humidity in the greenhouse is detrimental to the growth of the plants. Here are a few tips on how to maintain the right relative humidity:

- **Avoid overwatering your growing medium.** Too much watering is the beginning of trouble in the plants' root system. The humidity level in the greenhouse increases when there is too much water in the medium.

- **Ensure enough air circulation.** This will improve the ventilation in the greenhouse and invariably ensure the right humidity level.

To keep plants from succumbing to disease, humidity must be kept in check. High humidity content in greenhouse air increases plant condensation, hampering breathing. Moreover, high humidity is a breeding ground for rodents and fungal diseases of plants. The vapor pressure deficit (VPD) must be routinely measured and maintained at the optimum level of 0 to 1 psi for better management of humidity. VPD is an ambient humidity measure as opposed to the humidity at which water condensation starts.

SHADE

Shading is a temperature and light control device that uses shades or blinders that are automatically operated. The curtains close when there is too much sunshine during the day or when it is required to maintain warm temperatures at night in the greenhouse. An internal temperature sensor detects and triggers the opening or closing of the shades.

The sun in summer can really scorch your plants, especially in a greenhouse. It is advisable to have shades fitted to the outside that can be easily rolled into place as necessary.

BENCHES

They not only provide the extra spacing in which you need to work, but can also prevent you from bending too much. Looking for a ventilated shelving system that provides good drainage of water and circulation of air is a good idea.

Specifically, lights are required to provide your plants with photosynthesis up to 24 hours a day. Now, what's a greenhouse point if you don't have the winter option to grow seasonal veggies? Look at the latest fluorescent light designs that have recently reached the famous HID lamps.

While it is smart for all greenhouses to employ screens or shade cloth to reduce the heating impact of sunlight, it is absolutely critical for a free-standing greenhouse. A free-standing greenhouse is usually a large structure, so it takes longer for the heat to build up to a damaging level. However, because it is so large and the air mass inside is so hard to move, it takes much longer to evacuate that heat to safe levels.

A shade cloth or screen will block a certain amount of light from entering. This limits catastrophic heating, while also protecting the leaves of a tender seedling from sun-scald.

Shade cloths come in different densities that block different amounts of light. Shade cloth with a 40 percent density, blocks 40 percent of the light. Shade cloth with a 60 percent density blocks 60 percent of the light. I prefer a white shade cloth with around a 40 percent density. If you are buying a free-standing greenhouse as a kit from a greenhouse supply, they will usually recommend the correct shade cloth density needed for that particular design.

Shade cloth is usually made of polyethylene covered by UV and helps with heating and condensation. They can all be cut to suit your greenhouse practice.

MIN/MAX THERMOMETERS

Measure both indoor and outdoor highs and lows. But what's important about these thermometers is that they will provide you with valuable information about how a given day's temperature fluctuates. This alone will tell you in your greenhouse if you need additional cooling or heating elements that can help you with your budget.

Watering systems have several services, primarily to help with plant growth, cooling, and moisture. Depending on the type of greenhouse you want, you usually want to keep the humidity around 60%.

You might want to invest in these for little more complicated greenhouses: when you're home, thermostats will support your greenhouse. Place a thermostat right in the middle of your greenhouse if you want to keep a worry-free temperature in your greenhouse. You would like to have a thermostat of heating and cooling close together and away from the sunlight, if possible.

If you are in cold climates, heaters are critical. Even if heat comes from sunlight during the day and is trapped in a greenhouse, it may not be enough. There are plenty of choices from electric heaters to gas heaters.

Evaporative air coolers are the best greenhouse cooling systems out there and usually come with a thermostat-built system. Water flows onto cooling pads, which reduces the circulating air temperature. Another useful feature is that they help filter bugs and dirt.

LIGHTING

While your electrician is fitting the heaters, it makes sense for them to fit lights for the greenhouse. The type of light will depend on what the purpose of the light is.

You can make space more aesthetically appealing by spotlighting particular areas in the greenhouse or more practical by adding strip lighting.

Again, you should not place the lights too close to the actual plants. An ultra-violet lamp can also be installed to provide better lighting in low-light conditions.

LED lighting is more expensive to install upfront, but a lot more energy efficient than incandescent bulbs or even your energy-saver bulbs.

It is also a good idea to place the light switches close to the entrance of the greenhouse so that you can find them easily in the dark.

IRRIGATION

If your greenhouse is in your garden, it is easy enough to pop down and waters it, but if it is at an allotment or you are on holiday, then watering becomes much trickier, putting your harvest at risk.

In the hottest weather, and more so in hotter climates, you will need to water your plants 2 or 3 times a day to keep them healthy no matter how good your cooling system is!

Chapter 6

EQUIPMENT AND TOOLS

GREENHOUSE EQUIPMENT

Greenhouse equipment is built most accurately; this segment contains numerous brands that supply world-class goods. Such goods are checked several times before they are released on the market to give you a hint. What distinguishes them is the quality at hand; if you choose a premium brand, this can certainly give you the required performance. Now, coming to the selection portion, this is the first step towards the main building. You are advised to choose well and to suit your needs. One wrong move, and in the building process, everything can go wrong. You also need to work on small details that can deliver the best output for you. There may be information about the greenhouse's design and other safety features.

Greenhouse equipment is made up of watering, lighting, exhausts, windows, and other equipment for construction. Buying all of this in the right way will help to save time and costs. Digital shopping can be considered a good choice for your needs. There are times were buying online will certainly give you all the long-term benefits. Each brand that the equipment of the supplier has its website, you can search on their website for greenhouse equipment and then finalize your vision. Price comparison can be made online, online purchases, and quotations from the internet can be used for price comparison. Selecting the right products will give you an added advantage.

Just know the brand you want to buy through; it should have consumer credibility. One should not go ahead without testing the brand as you may not know the type of service provided. Check on the website for customer evaluations, and this should give you an indication of the kind of customer service offered.

Greenhouse equipment should be produced in compliance with international standards; if the product complies with local standards, then the reliability and overall stability factor are expected to decrease. It would also help to make the order easy and affordable by looking for free delivery options. You don't need to waste time arranging for the purchased products to be transported. When it comes to such goods, choose wisely.

Therefore, buying greenhouse equipment is proving beneficial in the long run. With such equipment and tools, your dream greenhouse can be installed in no time. Make sure you have full permission from your greenhouse building architect. Beautify your landscape with state-of-the-artist greenhouses.

BUILDING GREENHOUSES ACCESSORIES WORTH HAVING

It's a good idea to install a ventilation system in your greenhouse. Plants can wilt under excess heat, so you're going to need a way out into the greenhouse to cycle fresh air. This is an emergency measure and can delete any discoveries you have made, but it can save the plants, which is better than starting from scratch. A chest or cabinet that is waterproof is a perfect place to store your equipment in the greenhouse. This will protect them against rust damage and moisture while reducing the need to move in and out of the greenhouse–behavior that will risk the greenhouse's temperature and health.

Have a few large sheets of plastic on hand to patch broken panes. Such temporary measures will keep the conditions of your greenhouse in check until you have a replacement stand. As you can see, a lot of things can be used to boost a greenhouse's functionality. There are things that we sometimes take for granted, which eventually give us a lot of support. You need to plan when constructing greenhouses to accommodate additional features, such as those shown above.

Building and running a greenhouse can be more than just a fun recreational activity you do in your spare time–it can help you financially (if you sell plants or produce) and safely (by eating healthy foods). Installing such main accessories will ensure that your greenhouse will provide you with maximum return and performance.

Vegetation thrives when the growth area, climate, and disease and pest protection factors are maintained at optimum rates. Accessories make it easier and quicker to know and manage these optimal conditions. These come at a high cost, but they may well be worth the returns.

Here are some useful greenhouse accessories to have:

Heaters

Heaters are the first greenhouse equipment you need to install in your greenhouse. This is because plants need to thrive at a specific temperature. It is particularly important if your greenhouse for plastic or glass is located in a cold area that gets colder during winter. The heaters come in many types as per your specifications, such as gas heaters, paraffin heaters, or electric heaters. It is essential to avoid blowing air directly on plants, and however, as it can be harmful, it is always beneficial for the heat (or cool air) at the level of the soil.

Climate Controls

Climate controls are also critical greenhouse devices, just like heaters. Depending on the season, a good climate control system can heat up or cool the greenhouse. It is recommended that you position your plants on benches so that even air circulation is provided. Heating and cooling thermostats, variable speed controls humidistat, cycle timers, and advanced controls are the various types of controls available on the market.

Ventilation Equipment

As the name suggests, this device helps manage the air in your garden so you can grow plants that usually don't thrive in your area. Choose from any of the following greenhouse ventilation devices, such as evaporative coolers, exhaust fans and shutters, automatic vent openers, and circulation fans, for proper air circulation in your greenhouse environment.

Misting Systems

Effective misting systems are useful in any greenhouse construction process to maintain optimal humidity and temperature, ensuring plants grow at the desired rate. There is a wide range of options such as sprinkler systems, misting systems, mist timers, and valves as well as water filters that are commonly used in institutional greenhouse-style installations.

Watering Supplies

As is evident, water supplies are the most critical part of taking care of even during the design of the greenhouse. From a wide range of water supplies such as plant watering systems, drip systems, qualified water hoses, water timers, and overhead watering systems, you can choose according to your specific requirements.

Irrigation System

Without water, plants cannot grow. An irrigation system will make it easier to distribute water to the greenhouse plants quickly and evenly. Combining customizable nozzles, overhead sprinklers, and field drip feeders would be the perfect irrigation method.

Downpipe Kits

You can save considerable watering costs by collecting the runoff of rainwater. Downpipe kits harness rainwater that will channel it to reservoirs that will then feed into the irrigation and/or cooling system of the greenhouse. The only catch is to ensure that the water is purified from soil or debris before being pumped into the irrigation or cooling system, as this may cause a blockage.

Greenhouse Shelving

If you put in your backyard a greenhouse, space is likely to be a major constraint. Greenhouse shelves ensure that the vertical area is used as much as possible. Shelving comes in various heights, a number of shelves, and materials for construction.

Growing Racks

Growing racks ensure a mini greenhouse is used effectively and easily. The racks shield plants from extreme weather impacts, while the zippers allow access to the seedlings.

Shade Cloth

Shades shield the plants from the harmful ultraviolet rays of the sun and also help regulate the greenhouse temperature. The shades can be manual or controlled by the sensor. For areas where sunlight and outside temperatures typically change rapidly, manual shades can be complicated.

Vent Openers

Reduce heating and air conditioning costs by installing winds at suitable locations. You can choose between natural and automatic ventilation, which is costly but more efficient and can be built into central heating or air conditioning system.

Chapter 7

GROWING IN THE GREENHOUSE

GERMINATION OF GREENHOUSE SEEDS

For the gardener, nothing gives us as much hope as a well-functioning greenhouse. There is always the possibility of a new life born of these small, lifeless fragments we call seeds. Add some water, heat, a good mix of soil and, there you have it, a new life. If only it were that simple. The greenhouse provides the ideal environment for plant growth, but it also provides the ideal environment for disease proliferation. With care, a little knowledge, and the right tools, spring can spend all year in your greenhouse.

PLANTING MEDIUM

A good germination medium for greenhouse seed is usually composed of a combination of vermiculite, perlite, peat, coarse sand, treated bark, or expanded shale. However, there are commercial mixes that offer several advantages over domestic media. These mixtures are certified free of weeds, insects, and diseases. They are convenient and ready to use directly from the bag and already contain a small amount of fertilizer incorporated into the mixture to keep the seedlings for 2 to 4 weeks. The smaller the seeds for planting, the better the soil should be.

CONTAINERS

Containers used for seed germination in greenhouses should be sterile. Constant high humidity and greenhouse heat provide ideal conditions for the development of plant diseases. Flatbeds, 2 to 3 inches deep, with holes in the bottom for drainage are the best type of container for most seeds such as beans or grain. The seedlings will grow rapidly and absorb excess water.

SOWING SEED

The container is filled with germination media up to ½" from the top. The surface is moistened and the excess water is evacuated. The seeds are evenly distributed on the top of the medium. Planting depth is indicated on most seed packets. Seeds sowed too deep cause congestion and little growth. Tiny seeds, such as petunias or impatiens, are left untouched or covered with a very thin layer of vermiculite. The seed fragments are covered with coarse sand or sphagnum vermiculite. Water the new plant taking care not to disturb the surface material layer.

TEMPERATURE AND MOISTURE

It is best to keep seedlings at the temperature recommended for the species, indicated on the seed package. Most seeds germinate at temperatures between 70 and 80°F in 7 to 10 days. To accelerate germination, a heating cable, available at the garden center, is set at a temperature of 70 to 85°F and placed under jars with seeds. High humidity is required for seed germination, preferably 100%. Manual irrigation is best for small batches of pots with seeds, being careful not to disturb the surface of the soil. For large plantings, use a sprinkler with a flow tube.

MAINTENANCE OF STERILE CONDITIONS

The sterility of the containers, supports, and tools used for seed germination is the most important factor for successful growth. New seedlings are particularly susceptible to plant diseases, such as fungi and bacteria, which can persist for a long time in pots, soil, reservoirs, and tools, and then kill a complete planting in a few days. Containers must be new or disinfected in a 10% bleach solution for 5 minutes before use. Usually, a sterile mix is your best option and the habitat should contain only sterile components. All instruments or tools that touch the floor can be easily sterilized in a 10% bleach solution. The benches and greenhouse boards should be disinfected in the same way that the trays and tools to ensure sufficient airflow between the trays.

CHECK THE TEMPERATURE

Tomatoes grow best at day temperatures of 21 to 27°C (70 to 80°F) and 16 to 18°C (60 to 65°F) at night. Be sure to maintain these temperatures in the greenhouse for several months before planting.

Ideally, set the temperatures at the low end of this range on rainy days and increase them to a maximum (or even a little higher) on sunny and bright days.

Select a Variety of Tomatoes

There are thousands of varieties of tomatoes, so it is best to contact local producers for detailed information. However, some guidelines and tips apply to all regions: If you run out of space, plant a "certain" variety that stops at a certain height.

Choose a traditional tomato that can grow on any well-drained material.

Pearl wool or rock wool bags are the smallest options in many areas. Some manufacturers prefer a 1:1 mixture of peat and vermicelli.

Buy some sterile soil or make your own. Never use soil or compost from your yard or garden without sterilization. Choose this option if you do not want to install an irrigation system.

Install an irrigation system

Install drip tubes to supply water to each plant. A tube-connected fertilizer injector can also automate fertilization. Tomatoes are easy to grow in a hydroponic system.

Planting

Fill a starter tank with dirt. Wash the pan with soap and water to disinfect it. Fill the pot with one of the potting mixes described above. If using the soil from the ground, make sure it is sterile.

If you use a soilless mixture, you also need a good nutrient solution.

Drill a 6 mm. (¼") hole in each container. Plant one seed in each hole. Lightly cover with compost soil. Plant 10 to 15% more seeds than you want. Later you will eliminate the weakest seedlings.

Moisten with water or nutrient solution. Use simple groundwater or seedling nutrient solution for soilless mixes. In both cases, water until the mixture is moist enough to form a pool, with a few drops drained. Water regularly to keep the mixture moist.

A 5:2:5 nutrient solution containing calcium and magnesium is ideal. Dilute the solution according to the instructions on the label.

Keep the containers in front of a warm window. Do not bring seeds into the greenhouse until they have germinated to avoid diseases and parasites. Make sure there is enough sunlight and maintain the temperature between 24 and 27°C (75 and 80°F) throughout the day.

Move them to the full sun once all the seedlings are growing. This usually lasts 5 to 12 days.

Transplant into larger containers. Transplant the plants in small pots in a greenhouse approximately two weeks after emergence. After six to eight weeks, or once the plants reach 10 to 15 cm (4 to 6"), transplant larger plants into pots or bags. A typical plant needs about 1 to 2 cubic meters of space (3.7 to 7.5 gallons or 14 to 28 liters). Some varieties will produce less fruit if they are grown in small pots.

If you see insects, molds, or disease spots on a plant, do not bring them into the greenhouse. You risk contaminating the entire crop.

Adjust the levels. Before the final transplant, you may want to check and adjust the pH of the soil, which ideally ranges between 5.8 and 6.8. If your soil is too acidic, add about 1 tbsp. (5 ml.) of hydrated lime per gallon (3.8 L) of soil. In addition to increasing the pH, add calcium to prevent the rotting of flowers later. If not, choose only calcium-containing fertilizer and apply it every week or two.

Chapter 8

HOW TO GROW PLANTS AND FLOWERS

The Earth and life, in general, would have become quite boring and monotonous if it were not for flowers—magical, colorful buds that are mesmerizing to the eyes and scintillating to the nostrils.

Even though green is a color that comforts the eye, you might not like the sight of an all-green greenhouse (even though the name suggests it should be green) and would prefer to have a variety of flowers growing inside to make you want to go to the greenhouse every hour of every day and take in the various scents and sights to be found.

Here is the good news: armed with a greenhouse, you can grow a variety of popular flowers, as long as you take care of the sunlight, water, and soil requirements for each! Let me take you through these varieties and the tips and tricks you should follow to get the best-looking flowers growing in your greenhouse.

AMAZON LILIES

Standing tall at up to 2 feet from the ground, Amazon lilies will add a comforting and sweet aroma to the atmosphere inside your greenhouse, along with a sight of white petals that is pleasant to the eyes.

To safely grow healthy lilies, you need to take care of the temperature, moisture, and sunlight. Because it is a tropical flower, you must keep the atmosphere around these flowers at 70 degrees F to not cause them to wither and die. Other than that, avoid watering the flower too much and ensure that it gets at least 8 hours of sunlight daily. As long as you take care of these guidelines, your Amazon lilies will be a sight to behold!

AFRICAN VIOLETS

Despite the name, African violets come in a variety of colors and so are an excellent addition to any greenhouse if you want to make the sight of it fully attractive colors. African violets are not very demanding in terms of conditions when it comes to their growth, so all you need to make sure is to have low-nutrient soil and high humidity in the vicinity where these are growing.

One important note: unless you want to ruin the diverse colors of these violets, avoid sprinkling any water onto the petals or making them wet because it will take away the color from the flower.

An advantage of growing this flower is that you can simply use cuttings from an existing plant to grow more—that's how easy it is to reproduce these flowers.

CHENILLE PLANTS

The name of this 'flower' may have surprised you—why is it called the chenille plant? This is because this flower is more like a plant and less like a standard flower. The reason it gets lumped into the flower family is that it has long outgrowths (that can grow up to six feet tall) that are red and look a lot like the tail of a cat (that's why it is also known as "cat's tail").

If you're interested in adding a bright red tinge to your greenhouse, consider planting chenille plants. Just make sure you provide them with adequate sunlight or else you won't get the red color that makes them so popular.

CHINESE HIBISCUS

The Chinese hibiscus are flowers that bloom gloriously and are a sight that would freeze many rights in their tracks, but there's a bittersweet element to this marvel as well—these flowers bloom for 24 hours at a maximum and then wilt and die, no matter what you do.

Still, it is worth growing them in your greenhouse garden, because the 4" span of its flowers and petals will fill your greenhouse with a beautiful sight for one single day. On top of that, these come in a variety of colors including red, pink, white, orange, and yellow, so imagine having a rainbow living inside your greenhouse for one full day. There's just one thing you need to keep in mind: the Chinese hibiscus are incredibly sensitive to sudden drops in temperature, so you must make sure the temperature inside your greenhouse is maintained at a warm level at all times.

ROSES

Roses need no introduction—these flowers have long been associated with romance and love, and are popular in all parts of the world. An interesting fact is that these are particularly suited to greenhouses because of their sensitive nature.

If you want to grow roses in your greenhouse, the one thing you must make sure is that the temperature is maintained at a stable 70 to 80°F, or else your roses will either not blossom at all, or wilt away quickly and die. Other than that, roses also need plenty of sunlight so place them in a position inside your greenhouse which receives a lot of sunshine every day.

Finally, because of the many varieties available, it is best to speak to your local nursery about the varieties they are selling you and understand the custom requirements of that specific variety so that your roses turn out to be healthy and beautiful!

ORCHIDS

Even though I didn't design this list in an order of ascending difficulty, we have arrived at the flower that, as its precious beauty may suggest, is one of the most sensitive and difficult to grow.

If you want to grow orchids, you must have a greenhouse where you can regulate and maintain the desired temperature with great accuracy and consistency.

This is because orchids will fail to grow and end up withering away in both colder and warmer temperatures than the ideal range.

So, during the day, ensure that the temperature remains inside a range of 70 to 80°F, and it remains inside the range of 50 to 60°F to get the best out of your Orchids.

As long as you take care of this important guideline and provide it a humid atmosphere, you can be sure that your orchids will grow safely and healthily and make you proud!

Chapter 9

HOW TO GROW VEGETABLES

A greenhouse is excellent for starting your seeds indoors before it's safe to plant seedlings outside. And this will enable you to jump-start on the growing season. Nevertheless, you need to harden off the plants so that the change in temperature does not kill them. Those plants that spend the longest time to reach harvest are the best to grow in a greenhouse. For instance, tomatoes work better than do radishes and lettuces. Both radishes and lettuces are short period crops, you can plant all three though. Tomato is better since it takes much longer to turn out a harvest. The following are considered some of the best vegetables to grow in a greenhouse:

- Tomatoes

- Artichoke

- Peas

- Cauliflower

- Kale

- Broccoli

- Arugula

- Collard Greens

Some crops work better in a cold frame instead of a greenhouse, and those include:

- Herbs that love cool weather

- Carrots that don't transplant well

- Salad greens such as lettuces

If you plan to grow the whole crops in the greenhouse, then these plants are the best. Plants such as corn that are wind-pollinated may not yield well. If you intend to grow your entire plant in the greenhouse, make sure you take the challenges of pollinating into consideration when choosing the design of the structure.

SUCCESSIVE PLANTING

A perfect tool for successive growing is a greenhouse. This equipment can be used to start seeds four to eight weeks before planting. For example, in my area, I sow tomatoes in the middle of March so that they become healthy seedlings and a foot tall or so. Then take them from the seed tray where they germinate to 4-inch containers.

I start heirloom tomatoes seeds 8 weeks earlier than the expected planting date, and I transfer them to one-gallon pots before transplanting them into the ground in mid-May or early June.

When successive gardening is applied, you will foresee the date of harvest for plants and then get ready for your next plant while the current plants are still growing and budding. The essence of this is to make the most use of the smaller growing space of a container to begin your next plant. It means you're raising two gardens at once, but since the following sets of plants are small, they need less space. Going by this, you will gain about a 6 to 8 weeks decrease in time between one harvest and the next. Therefore, a greenhouse is a tool that helps you boost the overall yield or produce all through your growing season. Almost all plants you will be growing in your garden are the "best" plants to be grown in greenhouses If successive gardening is what you intend. Only those plants such as carrots that don't transplant well are the exceptions.

GREENHOUSE GARDENING IN COLD CLIMATES

In most parts of the world and the United States, it's either the growing season is shorter or winter is freezing. For these two circumstances, greenhouses are the perfect growing instrument. As I've said earlier, not all plants that thrive in a greenhouse in all season of the year. Some plants require direct sunlight than others, but using glow light can make up for the lighting needs. Grow lights were first used by the aquarium manufacturing company to grow plants and corals or home aquariums. Due to the changes to the legal marijuana stand, grow lights are now available at more affordable prices almost everywhere. This implies that you can make up for the drop in direct sunlight by using the artificial lamp for locations with a short growing season.

Shorter days and fewer nights also affect the colder growing weather. For most plants, it's the decrease in light that causes setbacks, but the temperature is another factor. These are the reasons while a greenhouse becomes an instrument to make up for both a decrease in warmth and a reduction in lighting.

In both scenarios, those plants that require a warmer growing climate and additional lighting are the best plants to grow in a greenhouse. They can range from vegetables that you intend to grow all-year-round, to citrus trees in pots. For year-round growing, it is ideal to opt for plants that grow well in reduced light in the months of winter and where the plants would not be transplanted outside. Some of the plants are:

- Roots such as potatoes, carrots, and other cold-loving plants

- Brassicas such as cauliflower, broccoli, and kale

- Herbs

- Lettuces and other greens

- Garlic

- Onions

- Peas

Another method to make up for the cooler temperature in late fall, winter, and early spring is to make the most use of a heating technique with your greenhouses. It will allow you to grow crops (such as basil) that are sensitive to a decrease in temperature.

Gardeners use different types of heating sources to keep their greenhouses warm. The natural way to keep your greenhouse warm is solar radiation. But when the sunlight goes down, the warmth in the greenhouse follows suit. A line of plastic jugs filled with water inside the structure may be all it requires to heat your greenhouse during the night.

Consider installing a heating device if you desire to have more control over the interior temperature of your greenhouse. Both gas and electric heaters are examples of systems that enable you to have more control over the fluctuations of the temperature of the structure. You can also use heat lighting methods but may be costly, and anything electric will go down when there is a power outage except you have a generator.

Several DIY heating project types are beneficial. Old cast iron wood stoves are easy to install. Inverted flower pot radiator heaters are also great and easy to build. This implies that there are many available options when it comes to heating your greenhouse, which allows you to make the most use of the benefits of greenhouses in different unfavorable climates.

Chapter 10
HYDROPONICS IN THE GREENHOUSE

WHAT IS HYDROPONICS?

Hydroponics is a system that uses a nutrient-rich water solution to grow plants without soil. The plants have their roots submerged in the water which is then mixed with various nutrients and minerals. The effects on the plant's growth are very similar to those when they are grown in soil, but there are some differences worth noting.

BENEFITS OF HYDROPONICS

One major benefit of hydroponics is that it conserves water by using less than what would be needed if using other techniques like conventional farming or container gardening with inert media such as peat moss or potting mix. Another benefit is that the plants' roots are not disturbed by working soil and can therefore stay healthier. Another benefit is that the plants have the opportunity to grow much faster than the same plants grown in soil.

DOWNSIDES OF HYDROPONICS

One downside of hydroponics is that it can be a little more difficult to keep the water evenly saturated throughout each plant's root system, which may cause problems if used on large gardens or with multiple types of plants. Some nutrients may not be readily available to these plants, depending on the type of hydroponic system used. For example, in some cases, plants may have too much nitrogen and need to be removed from their nutrient solution. Another downside is that long-term maintenance and upkeep of the system may be a little more difficult. For example, you will have to check in on each plant about every other day or so to dissipate any excess heat from the lights to maintain proper temperature and humidity levels.

WHAT KIND OF PLANTS SHOULD I GROW IN MY HYDROPONICS SYSTEM?

When it comes to deciding which type of plant you would like to grow in your hydroponics system, there are a few main categories: flowering plants, herbs, vegetables, or fruits. There are many different varieties of these plants and if you don't see what you want, try asking one of the various garden stores on our website or at your local home improvement center.

Find a supplier that has all the supplies you need and can help to answer any questions you may have about hydroponics.

HYDROPONICS: WHAT ARE THE CHALLENGES?

Before you start setting up your system, there are a few important things to consider. The first is the type of plants that you would like to choose for your garden and if they are appropriate for growing in hydroponics. Some types of plants are more difficult to grow in this system so it is important that you research which plants have been successfully grown using this technique. The second thing to consider is the size of your system. You need to make sure that you have room to set up your system and that your plants will fit in the space available without being crowded. The third thing to consider is the equipment that you have space for to use in your system. You will need to decide what kind of lighting, water pumps, filtration systems, and other necessary items you can fit into your given space.

The types of plants that can be grown using hydroponics are virtually limitless! There are some plants that may be particularly well-suited for this kind of growing environment because they require less maintenance, but even with these plants, proper care must be given, or else problems could arise. Some examples of these kinds of plants include peppers, tomatoes, or strawberries.

WHAT IS THE BEST LIGHT TO USE?

For growing plants in a hydroponics system, you will need to have some sort of lighting to help simulate the sun. Plants obviously require sunlight in order to survive and grow and it is actually not necessary for you to use the same kind of light that comes naturally from the sun. There are many different kinds of lights that can be used for hydroponic growing, but most people will choose one of three kinds of lighting: fluorescent, LED, or HID. Fluorescent lights are commonly used by beginning gardeners because they are very inexpensive and do not put out much heat which can dry out plants. LED lights are relatively new and this kind of lighting provides a lot of benefits. LED lights can be used for growing plants indoors as well as outdoors and are much more heat resistant than fluorescent lights. HID lights, or high-intensity discharge, lights contrast greatly with LED lights in that they put out a lot of light energy at a very low wattage.

WHAT KIND OF WATER SHOULD I USE?

With plants in hydroponics systems, you will have to make sure that you have the correct kind of water for your specific type of plant. You should research what the preferred water is for your type of plant and then monitor it to make sure it stays fresh. If your water contains too much or too little nutrients, that may cause problems with the health of your plant.

WHAT KINDS OF NUTRIENTS DO I NEED?

When you are setting up a hydroponics system, one thing you will have to decide is what kind of nutrients and minerals will be used in the water. This will vary greatly depending on your type of plant and if you are growing vegetables, fruits, herbs, or flowers. Usually, there is a grow shop nearby that can supply you with the right combination of nutrients for your specific kind of plant, but you should make sure to ask questions so that you know exactly what is going into your system.

HOW DO I SET UP A HYDROPONICS SYSTEM?

When it comes to setting up a hydroponics system at home, the process can be a little bit harder than just planting in soil and forgetting about it. Hydroponic systems require daily attention because they need to be prepared each day for the growth of the plants in order to make sure they have enough food, water, and light. Here are some quick steps to follow in order to set up a hydroponic system at home:

- Find the right space for your system

- Purchase the necessary equipment for your system

- Prepare the water and insert it into the growing bed

- Set up your lighting

- Start planting seeds

- Establishing soil

Chapter 11

PESTS AND DISEASES AND HOW TO FIGHT THEM

MOST COMMON PESTS FOUND INSIDE A GREENHOUSE AND HOW TO CONTROL THEM

Greenhouse pests can be divided into three categories. These include sap-feeding insects, pollen feeders, and leaf eaters (like caterpillars and slugs). Most pest prevention techniques help deter common insects.

However, some pests are harder to control. It's why your greenhouse plants require constant monitoring and additional protection for successful cultivation.

Let's have a look at the common bugs you might come across during greenhouse gardening:

Sap-Feeding Insects

Sap-feeding insects have special sucking (and piercing) mouthparts. They use it to feed on plant cells (like mesophyll) and sap. Some common sap-feeding insects found inside the greenhouses include aphids, mites, mealybugs, scale insects, and whiteflies.

Plant Damage

Sap-feeding insects drain the liquid part of plants along with the nutrients and minerals it transports. In turn, this strips the essential nutrients required for plant growth. It also causes plants to become severely dehydrated.

They are known as one of the most destructive greenhouse gardening pests.

That is because pest damage from these insects is often undetectable during the initial phases of the infestation. Eventually, you might notice a shiny, translucent look in the affected plants. They will also feel sticky.

Without intervention, the sticky plants may develop a black, sooty appearance. It marks the arrival of a fungus (called sooty mold) that grows on honeydew (i.e., sugary droppings) excreted by sap-feeding insects. The sweet droppings might attract ants too.

Other signs include:

•   Leaf stippling (i.e., spotted appearance)

•   Yellow leaves and discoloration

•   Leaf curling (i.e., distorted leaves, with edges curled inwards)

•   Galls (i.e., plant tissues look swollen due to abnormal outgrowths)

Aphids

Aphids (often called plant lice) are small, slow-moving insects. Greenhouse infestation begins when 1 or 2 winged insects come inside through an open vent or door. Their high reproductive cycle and resistance to most insecticides make aphids a threat to greenhouse plants.

Aphids are known to form clusters of colonies on sap-containing parts of host plants (i.e., leaves and stems). These insects extract plant sap by piercing into the target area and using their beak-like mouths to suck.

They typically attack the young leaves of most food crops, fruit trees, and flowering plants except for garlic and chives. Aphids feed on the tenderest part of the host plant, usually found under the leaf. Their presence attracts ants and encourages mold infestations due to their sugary droppings. Besides this, aphids can transmit plant diseases.

Pest Control

Most gardeners recommend running multiple insecticide applications to manage aphid invasion. We recommend two-three applications conducted between 3-7 day gaps. You can alter the schedule depending on the severity of the situation.

Additionally, using alternate insecticides for each cycle can delay resistance against specific formulas. In turn, this maximizes the chances of achieving desirable results. You can also use neem oil and diatomaceous earth to control aphid infestation.

Mites

Mites (or spider mites) have a distinctive dusty-like appearance. These microscopic arachnids are distant cousins of ticks and spiders. They reside in the leaves' underside, like most sap-sucking pests, of ornamental plants, shrubs, and fruits.

Like aphids, they reproduce rapidly, causing severe crop damage.

Spider mites pierce the cell wall to suck sap and succulent plant tissues. In turn, this causes spots as most of the nutrients inside the host plant get drained. After a while, nutrient deficiency leads to yellow spots. These patches might appear throughout the affected leaf/stem. Without intervention, these plants might die.

Other noticeable signs of these tiny pests include curled leaves, deformed leaves, and a trail of fine web-like silk strands.

Pest Control

Pesticide resistance makes them difficult to control mites. They are also challenging to eliminate due to their hidden locations and microscopic size. These factors make repeated insecticide application necessary to destroy mite eggs and their population.

Gardeners recommend spraying pesticides on the lower and upper sides of the affected leaves. Two to three applications scheduled between five-day gaps generally improve effectiveness. Introducing natural predators like ladybugs and lacewings also helps.

Whiteflies

Whiteflies resemble small moths, but they look like moths that are dusted with white powder. They are not actual flies but tiny sap-sucking insects with wings. Adult whiteflies only flutter away if their breeding and feeding grounds are disturbed. Otherwise, they prefer to stay under leaves to suck the succulent stems and sap continuously.

They mainly attack ornamental flowering plants such as hibiscus, gerbera daisy, poinsettia, and geranium. Besides this, they are found in vegetable patches. Usual feeding sites include tomatoes, eggplants, and cucumbers.

Like all other sap-suckers, whiteflies consume plant juices by piercing into sap-filled cells. Common signs of whiteflies include discolored leaves, sooty mold, honeydew droppings, and wilting. Severe infestations might lead to crop reduction and plant death.

Pest Control

Whitefly removal revolves around biological and chemical control. Garlic sprays, neem oil, insecticidal soaps, and sticky traps placed on fruit trees are commonly used for pest control. Applications are spaced out between two-five days, depending on the severity of the infestation.

Pesticide resistance can be a concern. It is strongly advised to switch between insecticides to improve efficiency.

Apart from this, you can introduce beneficial insects and natural predators to greenhouses. Standard choices include whitefly parasites, lacewings, ladybugs, dragonflies, and hummingbirds. Most of these predators work well during the initial infestation stage as they feed on whitefly eggs and immature larva.

Nevertheless, their presence does deter reproduction rates. In turn, this facilitates other pest control methods.

Pollen Feeders: Thrips, Shore Flies, and Fungus Gnats

Pollen-feeding insects are small, often winged creatures. This category includes thrips, shore flies, fungus gnats, and small flies. These insects hover around flowers, often consuming nectar and helping with plant pollination. These insects leave traces of black feces and discarded exoskeletons wherever they go.

Plant Damage

Adult insects are nothing but a nuisance, but their larvae can be dangerous for plant growth. The immature pests feed on overwatered roots and inhibit nutrient intake.

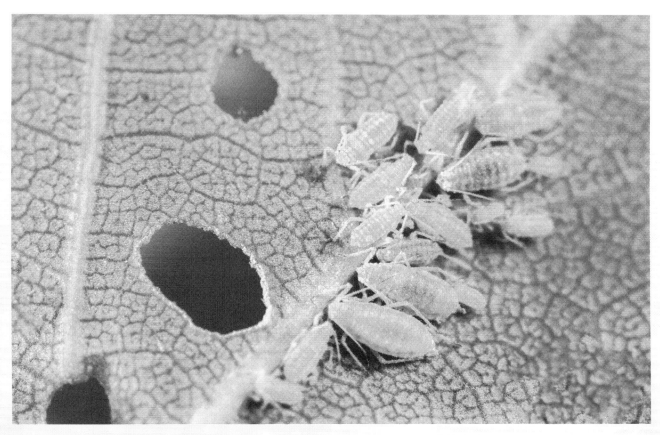

Common signs of infestation include:

• Yellow speckled leaves or silvered appearance

• Spotted flower petals

• Distorted fruits

• Visible black spots/droppings

• Some spotting on flowers

- Wilted leaves

- Scarred roots

- Reduced yield

Moreover, you will notice a swarm of mosquito-like insects flying over infected plants and larvae present at the back of infested leaves.

Pest control for pollen feeders works in the same way as sap-sucking insects.

Slugs and Caterpillars

Caterpillars and slugs might make an occasional appearance inside the greenhouse. They are categorized as defoliators (i.e., leaf eaters). They feed on young, succulent plants with tender leaves and juicy sap of seedlings, vegetables, flowers, and more. The most distinctive sign of these notorious pests is half-chewed leaves and bite marks.

Unlike other pests, they are visible to the naked eye. Their sluggish movement makes them detectable and easier to catch compared to other problems.

Plant Damage

These pests often attack plants at night, leaving trails of slime in the affected areas. Use a flashlight to check the underside of leaves when you search for them.

Other signs include:

- Big, ragged holes on leaves, vegetables, bulbs, flowers, and other parts of your greenhouse plants

- Leaves with bite marks

- No leaves on seedlings

Overall, their presence leads to damaged crops and reduced yield.

Pest Control

Their size and slow movement make pest control relatively easier if the infestation gets detected early. All you have to do is pick and toss these pesky pests into a bucket filled with soapy water. You can also use some insecticidal soap/spray to kill them off.

You can also use homemade pest repellants on them or neem oil to eliminate potential threats. Make sure that leaves are thoroughly washed to remove eggs and larvae.

3 COMMON GREENHOUSE PLANT DISEASES

There are 3 types of major plant diseases that you might experience during greenhouse gardening. These include fungal infections, viruses, and bacterial diseases.

The diseases emerge when healthy greenhouse plants contact carriers (i.e., sick plants, contaminated soil medium, and vector insects). Other sources include unclean irrigation water or air-borne diseases.

Here is a closer look at each plant disease type:

Fungal Infection

Fungal infections such as powdery mildew, root rot, and phytophthora might spread inside the greenhouse. High humidity and high moisture levels are often the leading cause of fungal growth. That's why; you must control moisture levels on leaves and stems. Also, do not overwater your plant. They might get waterlogged.

Visible signs of fungal growth include:

- Wilting

- Fuzzy lumps on leaves and stems

- Collapsed roots

- Yellowish tinge or complete discoloration

Most fungal infections target surface areas like leaves and stems. They are easy to cure. Neem oil and disinfectants are preferable choices for fungal removal. In severe cases, discard the affected area or uproot the infected plant to minimize spreading.

Bacterial Disease

There are four common categories of bacterial diseases (i.e., wilt, soft rot, necrosis, and tumors). They are grouped according to the severity of plant damage and symptoms. Blight, canker, crown gall, citrus canker, and blackleg are some known bacterial infections.

These diseases spread in numerous ways. They can be carried by insects, birds, a strong gust of wind, sometimes through contaminated water/tools. That's why we recommend sterilizing tools and using filtered water whenever you do gardening chores.

The common signs of bacterial infection in plants include:

•   Spotted leaf

•   Rotten fruits and vegetation

•   Wilting

•   Galls and overgrowths

•   Cankers and scabs, indicating erosion

•   Specks and blights

•   Distorted stems and leaves

In short, your plants will look sticky and gummy when they get sick. It's advised to quarantine them or remove them right away. Some gardeners suggest uprooting them and destroying them quickly before the disease spreads to neighboring crops.

Virus

Several plant-related viruses can destroy greenhouse crops and inhibit growth. They are either air-borne, water-borne, or through vectors. Common virus carriers include aphids and thrips.

Most viruses attack specific species or plant. You should monitor susceptible plants closely to detect signs of infection.

Signs and symptoms of plant virus include:

- Curling or rolling of affected leaves

- Mosaic-like patterns on leaves

- Spotting and marbling

- Discoloration causes green leaves to turn yellow

Prevention methods include quarantine for all new saplings and plants before placing them with the remaining crops. You should also sterilize your plant tools and equipment before use. In addition, place mesh covers with tiny holes during bug season to mitigate risks.

Chapter 12

HOW TO GROW HERBS

Herbs make great additions to all sorts of dishes and often it is hard to beat out the taste of a fresh herb. Their flavors are simply much more potent.

Growing herbs can be a frustrating process if you live somewhere where climatic conditions are either way too cold or scorching hot. That's because they won't survive in those types of environments. A greenhouse eliminates the climatic issue for you and allows you to create the perfect environment to grow and protect your fresh herbs. The greenhouse will both extend the season of growth for your herbs and give you a wider variety of herbs that you can grow. You want to make sure that your greenhouse is set up to have the right amount of shade and moisture for your herbs.

One of the biggest reasons that herbs fail to grow is because they don't get enough water. While the point of the greenhouse is to provide your plants with the best sunlight and climatic conditions, remember that there are some plants that need shade. Herbs are one of those plants that will require shading during the day. Especially during the hot afternoon sun, some greenhouses have shady areas in their roofs; other greenhouses are equipped with a shading system to give the plants that need it some shade.

There are a variety of herbs that are well suited to greenhouses; however, your best herbs will be the annuals. These herbs are often too sensitive to grow in outdoor areas. However, you can also grow any herb you wish to cultivate in your greenhouse.

The best greenhouse herbs are:

- Basil

- Chives

- Dill

- Chamomile

- Cilantro

- Parsley

- Mint

PARSLEY

Like so many other plants out there, parsley has several different varieties to it. Which variety you grow is up to you and what you want to use parsley for. You might have already noticed 1 or 2 types of parsley on the shelves of your local grocery store.

- Curled-leaf parsley is what you normally come into contact with. It is used in many dishes and is mostly known as a garnish for finished plates or in a delicious green salad.

- Root parsley is less common; however, chefs know it well for uses in soups and casseroles. It can even be steamed and eaten that way.

- Broad-leaf parsley is commonly named "Italian parsley". Many people can mistake it for cilantro but there is a distinctive difference in taste and look upon closer inspection of the herb. This is a sweet herb and is better suited to cooking recipes than as a garnish. It is a wonderful addition to soups.

Besides the tasty aspect of parsley, it too has several health benefits for the body. For example, this herb is full of vitamins A and C as well as iron. There are even home remedies that use parsley as a source to treat urinary tract infections and freshen breath. It is one of the most commonly used herbs when it comes to food and cooking dishes — particularly in Mediterranean cuisine. Those lovely pesto sauces you like to eat with your plates of pasta also have a mixture of parsley in them. When planting parsley in your greenhouse you can use containers, raised beds, hanging pots, or simply plant it in the ground.

You should preferably maintain roughly 7 inches between each seed as you plant them. Your soil for the parsley should be both rich in nutrients and moisture (remember not to soak the soil in water). Parsley seeds germinate slowly, so the best idea is to soak them in water one day before you plan on planting them. If you can soak the seed overnight in some warm water that is preferable. Pro tip: seeds that float should not be used for planting.

All other seeds can be used to plant. When your parsley begins to sprout make sure you do one of two things:

- Thin it out once it reaches roughly 2 to 3" in height.

- Transplant it to a bigger container where it has more space to grow. It helps to mulch around each parsley plant to ensure it stays moist and free of unnecessary weeds. Weeds only give your parsley competition and you don't want that. Like all plants, parsley is prone to some issues.

Rarely will pests and fungal diseases plague your parsley herbs, however, a caterpillar or two might crop upon them. Simply remove the caterpillar if you see it. The main disease to pay attention to with parsley is stem rot. Your parsley thrives in wet soil. Make sure that both before the period of germination and after the seed has begun to germinate you water the plant often to keep its soil wet. Once the sixth week has passed since germination began you can keep the soil moist and not as wet as before.

Your parsley will most likely mature roughly 11 weeks after you planted it in your greenhouse. To harvest the parsley, you need to pinch the leaves off of the main branch. Do this branch by branch and make sure that you leave the grown stem behind so that the herb can regrow.

DILL

Dill is a fun herb to grow in your greenhouse. With a little bit of attention, this fragrant herb will blossom in your garden and provide you the perfect herb to spice up those tasty fish dishes! Known as an annual herb, both dill seeds and the fresh herb itself are used to add flavor to many different types of cuisine. Like most other fresh herbs and vegetables, dill has an entire range of health benefits as well.

It is full of vitamin A and is used for anti-inflammatory purposes. Your dill seeds need to be sowed one-quarter inch into the soil and roughly 16-18 inches apart from one another. Dill can be planted in a container, but you need to make sure the container is at least 12 inches deep since the dill will grow a deep taproot. Roughly 15 days after the seed germinates and you plant the dill it will begin to sprout.

You can thin out the dill plant, this will allow it space to grow and flourish. The best time to thin them would be once they reach between one to two feet. Make sure no weeds smother the plant as it grows. You should avoid transplanting dill because it doesn't respond well to the shock of being transplanted. It is best if you keep it in the same container that you used to grow it from day one. Simply make sure the container is large enough. Dill can grow some long flower stems, in this case, simply provide the flowering herb with some stakes for support. Also, make sure that the place in your greenhouse is shielded from wind and airflow because the dill can be susceptible to windy breezes.

To have dill constantly available to you, the best way to manage that is to do successive planting as I mentioned earlier. Sow a few seeds at first and then have the next ones ready to plant whenever your harvest period for the dill begins. Thankfully dill is one of the tougher herbs and you don't have to spend a lot of time preventing diseases and pests from bothering it. It may still be susceptible to infections like root rot and leaf spot however, a clean greenhouse and proper ventilation will be your best combatants against that. The very first month you plant dill it will be a thirsty plant. It will need roughly four inches of water every second day during this time. If you don't water the plant enough then you won't produce enough herbs to satisfy your needs. When you harvest dill, you can harvest the entire plant basically. You can eat the stems, leaves, flower heads, and even the seeds of dill! Dill matures around 2 feet, however, once the herb is producing over five leaves that are healthy in shape and form you can start harvesting the herb. Scissors will be your best bet to cut off branches and stalks of dill.

BASIL

If you're looking for a step up from your beginner herb then you need to try basil. Basil can be a little bit more complicated than your average herb, however, the main reason it fails for most gardeners is a lack of proper water. Basil is a famous herb that is well known for its distinctive aroma. It is used in all types of cuisine, and even as garnishes in drinks. You need to regulate the light, moisture, and temperature that you grow your basil in. It likes nutrient-rich soil that

provides good soil aeration. Once you plant basil seeds you will typically see them sprout in a week and a half to two weeks. Luckily, basil is less finicky than dill and you can transplant it. Simply make sure that your sapling has five or more real leaves growing before you transplant it. Plant the seedlings roughly 4 inches away from each other so they can grow properly. Basil needs regular water so that it doesn't blossom early.

However, there's a fine balance between the right amount of water and overwatering. If the bottom leaves of your basil plant begin to wilt and turn yellow give it a break, it's letting you know that it has too much water. Always water your basil at the root because you don't want the leaves to get too wet as this can incite a fungal disease to grow. Basil does need about 6-8 hours of sunlight (or artificial light) to ensure that it grows properly. Alternatively, fluorescent light can be used in the lack of sunlight, however, you need to up its exposure to 8 to 10 hours. You want to make sure that you pinch any new young buds as they are appearing and remove them so that your current basil leaves will continue to flourish. In one year, the basil plant will demand roughly 53 inches of water from you to grow at its best rate.

Chapter 13
HOW TO GROW FRUITS

Many gardeners prefer to grow vegetables than they do fruits. However, if you're providing for your family then there are a great many reasons to provide them with homegrown fruit that is free from harmful chemicals and pesticides.

Because of the finicky climates that fruits require to grow, most gardeners decide to stop at strawberries and not venture much further into the world of fruits than that. However, there is still a wide variety of fruits that do well in a greenhouse that doesn't require a ton of attention to detail. I will go into detail with these specific fruits in one moment. The best fruits that you can try to cultivate in your greenhouse are:

- Raspberries

- Peaches

- Strawberries

- Grapes

- Melons

- Oranges

- Lemons

GRAPES

It is a common misconception that growing grapevine means you need high temperatures.

In a greenhouse it is possible to mimic temperatures that are higher than usual, however, you still want to maintain the right climate for all of your plants, not merely the grapes. If you select your variety of grapes with care, you can successfully grow them in your greenhouse.

When you are thinking of planting grapes, remember that they will need open and well-draining soil so that they grow to their best capacity. If their soil becomes clogged up with water, your crop won't grow as well as you want it to. You will also want a system of support for the grapevines to

grow on. The flowers on the vines will turn into fruit and that is what you are looking for.

Typically, this might take a year of growth before you see the fruits of your labor with the grapes, but it is well worth it. Throughout their year of growth, you will need to occasionally give them attention to make sure that they are growing healthily and that they are receiving the right amount of water at their roots.

Once you see that the fruit is starting to grow on your vines it is important to thin them out so that the grape has enough space to grow to its full potential. You can use scissors to make quick and easy work of this. Typically, you will work upwards from the bottom and take off all the smaller fruits.

Aphids, spider mites, and other insects are the biggest threats to your grapes. They need to be watched for any signs of these. Again, you can deter this from happening by ensuring a clean environment in your greenhouse and proper ventilation so no mildew spreads over your plant.

PEACHES AND NECTARINES

Who said you can't have your peach and eat it too? Whether your greenhouse is heated or cooled, you can grow both peaches and nectarines in your greenhouse garden. When selecting varieties of peaches for your greenhouse the Peregrine is a great option because it is self-fertile. For nectarines, Humboldt is a good variety to try and plant. The Hale's Early is also another excellent choice for peaches; however, you must keep in mind that this variety will require you to possibly mechanically pollinate to produce fruit.

There is a bit of time and hard work that goes into making sure these trees stay healthy, however, their products will certainly make up for your effort. The best way to maintain your fruit tree once it has grown is to make sure you prune it and guide the tree towards a fan-like shape. This ensures that all the fruit has enough space to develop and you will have an easier time harvesting it.

Peach and nectarine trees are good fruits to have a starter plant from that you purchase at a nursery. However, if you prefer to nurture it from a seedling be prepared for a long wait until the tree reaches maturity.

A side effect of growing these fruits in a greenhouse will be that their roots will be more compact as a result of spacing. Make sure they get watered frequently, particularly during their growing season so that they are well fed. If you have a variety that needs to be pollinated, you will need to help your plant with the pollination process. You can use a tool to do this or merely a fine brush where you paint the pollen lightly from flower to flower. It can become tedious work as pollination needs to be done every single day during the plant's flowering stage. During manual pollination

make sure you raise the humidity in your greenhouse to ensure success with your fruits.

THE CITRUS FAMILY

Greenhouses don't discriminate and this means that lemons, tangerines, and oranges can all be grown in a greenhouse. The lowest temperature they can stand is 55°F but that is still enough for the seeds to germinate luckily! Your greenhouse will probably be at a higher heat than that if you have a heating system to ensure that your other plants have the climate they need to grow happily.

You can grow these citrus fruits from pips, however, it can take a while, up to ten years, for the trees to begin producing their own fruit. That's why I highly recommend getting starter plants from a nursery or even using a cutting from another tree to speed up the process.

Many gardeners choose not to heat their greenhouses excessively during winter months due to the cost of heating, however, if you're able to maintain your greenhouse at roughly 50°F during the night in winters then your citrus trees still have a good chance of yielding fruit.

CONCLUSION

Gardening is one of the calmest and most calming hobbies. Most people work in their gardens and flowerbeds for hours. The greenhouse is one of the easiest ways to enjoy gardening. You will deal with your plants throughout the year with a greenhouse. Read about home greenhouses and how in your gardening you can get the most from them.

Which will you need in your backyard for a greenhouse? It will rely on what you expect to expand and how much you are prepared to spend. You get some very cheap greenhouse kits while you also have a greenhouse installed to your specifications and pay for it a little more.

Where should you start learning everything about home greenhouses? The first place to look is on the Internet. There are many websites dedicated to greenhouse planting, while some are specialized in greenhouses. This way, you will find plenty of details or visit a kindergarten that sells greenhouses.

There are different kinds of greenhouses available for your home. A greenhouse kit is available. If you just start in your greenhouse hobby, this is a good way to go. These are also available online. You will be able to build your own greenhouse and learn all about home greenhouses with these kits. You can get a pack for it, no matter what size you choose.

In many sizes and forms, greenhouses come. Each is unique in its own way and is suitable for the kind of plants you wish to grow. There are those designed for beginners and those made for the professional gardener. Whatever you choose will decide what you plan to grow and how you use a greenhouse will ultimately determine your buying.

If you choose one, you will want a robust greenhouse. You certainly don't want it to fly through the yard with high winds in the first storm. Make sure you select a reputable dealer and search in your greenhouse for some standard construction designs.

Make sure the greenhouse you choose has a lot of ventilation windows and is made long-lasting. You can usually choose models that are more inexpensive manually, or you can choose models that move up and down like house windows. All ventilation windows must have screens to avoid insects attacking you and your plants during the warmer months.

A portable greenhouse may be of interest to you. It's great for children who are interested in planting and watching things grow. This is also a good choice for people who rent their homes. When you pass, your greenhouse will easily be packed to go with you. The portable greenhouses are as effective as any other kind of greenhouse effect.

Were you aware that you could garden in your high-rise apartment on the veranda? If you want a lawn, but you felt you couldn't because you live in an apartment in town, you're in to have a treat. The indoor greenhouses are available to you. Both models are smaller than the larger ones and serve almost the same function and operate very well. These are great for the smaller courtyard gardens.

There are a couple of things you need to know about home greenhouses. You will need to learn a few supplies required to grow in a greenhouse. It's kind of like getting your house furniture. The first thing you will need for your new greenhouse is a table for plants. You will use any form of the outdoor table, or you can choose one provided by your greenhouse dealer.

Pot and flats holding your plants can be found in any kindergarten. Most of the plants you buy already come with your own. However, you will need all the supplies necessary if you are to start plants from seeds.

Combine a range of a number of potting soils. You will also need other forms of fertilizer for the plants you expect to grow. You can get tips on this in your local kindergarten or online.

The tools you need to learn about greenhouses will be relevant. You will need a number of small shovels and truffles in a greenhouse for your gardening activities. You'll also need gloves. Many soils and fertilizers can be pleasant on your skin, and some flowering plants such as roses do not have thorns.

Don't forget that you're going to need a greenhouse heater when it gets old outside. An outdoor greenhouse can be gardened throughout the year. A variety of heater models are available, which are only designed to heat a greenhouse. Normally, you will buy them for the same dealer you purchased your greenhouse.

There is a method available called hydroponics to those of you who know a bit about gardening in a greenhouse or even to those who still learn all about home greenhouses. This is a kind of cultivation that allows plants to grow like minerals and supplements in just water. No soil is used in a hydroponic cultivation process. This is a very popular way of growing plants in a greenhouse and was found to make crops like tomatoes and peppers very effective.

There is a lot to learn about home greenhouses, and you will learn much when you work in one yard. The fun of a greenhouse is to experiment and learn what you can and cannot grow.

APPENDIX

Primrose

Primrose is a garden flowering plant that is most commonly used as decoration. Their scents are used for making perfumes, soaps, and body lotions. They come in different shapes and sizes and colors. Though they are also extensively grown in the spring, they also grow in winter and are commonly found in bedding plants.

Grapes

Grapes are fruits that are extensively grown in the winter season. Grapes are vines and hence are easy to grow along rails, fences, and poles. American varieties are the most popular ones that grow very well in winters. European ones are usually ones to be avoided, as they are susceptible to winter burns, sunscalds, and mildew.

Onions and Shallots

Onion and shallots are vegetables that can be planted during the autumn season and can grow very well in winter. They usually take a long time to grow and hence will be harvested only much later. Spring onions are other vegetables in the family of onions that grow in the winter. Red onions are widely grown in the spring season due to their intense flavor and scent.

Broad Beans

Broad beans are a type of bean usually grown in the autumn months. These broad beans are also extensively grown in the winter seasons. They, too, require quite a bit of time to grow and hence are usually harvested around the spring season.

Witch Hazel

Witch hazel is a shrub that has a variety of uses. It is a deciduous plant and is used in several skincare treatments. It also produces pale yellow flowers that are also widely used, which bloom in winter. It is most commonly used around the plants as a border and its strong scent can ward off pests and insects.

Asparagus

Asparagus is widely grown in winter and the autumn variety, or, the Pacific variety, is a favorite to plant. They are also bedding plants and are very slow in their growth rate. They take about two years to grow before you can harvest their produce.

Peas

Peas are the most commonly grown winter plants. Planting them during the early winter season or the autumn season can give a production a few weeks earlier. Seeds of pea Kelvedon wonder and pea meteor are hardy winter crops that can withstand the adverse climatic conditions found in winter.

Camellias

Camellias are beautiful flowering plants that produce pink and red flowers. These are cultivable during the winter season and usually provide flowers all year long. The most commonly planted variety of camellias is the tea plants. However, there are several types. Hybrid varieties are also available these days.

Calendula

Calendulas are flowering plants that are extensively grown in the winter season. They come in oranges and yellow shades and are commonly used as decoration. The trick with growing great calendula is to ensure that the soil is well irrigated. Poor irrigation can damage calendulas. They also require good sunlight.

Oregano

Oregano is a hardy winter herb that is robust and can withstand adverse cold. They are usually cultivated as a seasoning for food and their aroma is also sued in several room sprays. Oregano has an aromatic feel to it and hence is used for treating cough and cold.

Thyme

Thyme is another robust and hardy herb that is grown in the winter. They can be cultivated in pots and they are small, busy, aromatic plants. They are used as a seasoning over winter food like stews, casserole, roasts, and so on. They are also used to relieve coughs, colds, and the common flu.

Sage

Sages are best grown in August. However, they are generally grown in winter as well. They require a little bit more care, though. They require a lot of sunlight and little water. Sage is generally robust and is used as a seasoning herb for casseroles, salads, and vegetables. It is also used for the treatment of the common flu.

Parsley

Parsley is also an herb that is hardy. Parsley can be grown in pots but requires lots of sunlight and moist soil to flourish. These herbs have excellent antioxidant properties and are rich in a variety of vitamins. While picking parsley, it is a rule of thumb to pick the outer leaves to extend the life of the plant.

Sprouts

Sprouts are plants that can be cultivated any time of the year. Traditionally they are indoor plants and are grown very quickly and require adequate sunshine. Sprouts can be developed by placing the sprout seeds in a jar that is covered with water and left overnight. The next day, wash the sprouts and repeat this process.

Lettuce

Lettuce is a potted plant, which requires good soil and adequate water. They are best grown in window boxes. It is best to use the loose-leaf variety of lettuce as they prolong the life of the lettuce plants. While other varieties, like iceberg lettuce, are required to be sown every few weeks to get an adequate supply.

Radishes

Radishes are extremely hardy root plants commonly used for salads and dishes. They can easily be harvested because they require just a month to grow. However, the seeds need to be planted frequently to account for the radish supply. They also can be grown in pots and require a little bit of sun.

Strawberries

Strawberries are delicious plants that can be potted in the winter season. There are three major varieties of strawberries and it is best to plant the ever-bearing variety to get products in the winter. These plants require replacement about every 2 to 3 years because they will produce less as they age.

Printed in Great Britain
by Amazon